Google+ Business Basics: The Jargon-Free Guide to Simple Google+ Marketing Success

LEWIS LOVE

Although the author and publisher have made every effort to ensure that the information in this book was correct at press time, the author and publisher do not assume and hereby disclaim any liability to any party for any loss, damage, or disruption caused by errors or omissions, whether such errors or omissions result from negligence, accident, or any other cause.

Copyright © 2013 Lewis Love

All rights reserved.

ISBN: 1495984125
ISBN-13: 978-1495984129

Come writers and critics who prophesize with your pen.

CONTENTS

	Acknowledgements	i
1	Introduction	1
2	Google+ and Social Media	7
3	Setting Up Your Google+ Account	29
4	Engaging on Google+	42
5	Advertising on Google	54
6	The Most Important Chapter	56
7	What Next?	65

I'd like to thank those who I have worked with, without whom this book wouldn't be what it is. In particular; Louise for doing my networking for me, Jade for taking the time to point out my mistakes, and Adcocky, Maki-Moo, La Barbe and McDaddy for keeping me busy!

INTRODUCTION

The last few years has seen an explosion in the amount of content shared through social services such as Facebook, Twitter and Google+. Although search engines treat socially shared links differently than other types of links, they notice them nonetheless. There is much debate among search professionals as to how exactly search engines factor social link signals into their algorithm, but there is no denying the rising importance of social channels. The last three years has seen social media move from an uncertain strategy to an undeniable force behind the success of start-ups and established businesses alike. Every marketer now has their finger on the pulse of social media, keeping up-to-date with the latest offerings from Facebook, Twitter and Google+. No one has benefited more than small business owners and start-ups though. Social media plays a pivotal role in these businesses and this book will look at why that is.

It's important to point out at this early stage that marketing is not purely about boosting your sales. Sure, increases in revenue is always nice, but marketing encompasses many more parts of your business than you possibly realise. Marketing, especially on social platforms, affects your customer services, product development, merchandising and retail arms. You need to keep this in mind when reading this book and implementing advice, both techniques drawn directly from here and from other resources.

My Style of Business and Who It Helps

I don't believe in "one size fits all" at the best of times but especially when it comes to business. I feel that business advice has to be tailored to the business and as such no one person or consultant can be an expert for every business. Or at least, they can't be the right expert.

I don't claim to be the best social media consultant for every business. In fact, I don't claim to be the best – full stop. I believe there's always more to learn and that's what makes, for me, the online world and social media so exciting. This being said, I do understand where my experience and expertise lies.

The businesses that I help the most and those who get the most out of my advice are those who occupy somewhat of a middle ground in their market. I don't work particularly well with businesses that compete on price. That's because one of my firm beliefs is that if you compete on price and someone comes and undercuts you you've got nowhere to go. It's a race to the bottom, and that is all you have got to compete with. Price. Poundland worked well, until the 99ps Stores came along.

On the other hand I don't always work too well with high end, luxury brands. It's a market that is difficult to define and as soon as you begin to market and educate the market surrounding the higher end products you by default actually lessen the luxurious nature of the products. Ironically, I have written and published articles about the paradoxical nature of luxury brands, and whilst that work was well received, it hasn't made me any better working within that environment.

Whilst there are experts out there that can offer advice for these two ends of the market it's not where I sit. Where I sit is in the middle. The businesses that compete on service rather than price. Those that offer excellent products at a fair price. They might have some more luxurious offerings yet they don't distinguish themselves as luxury brands.

When it comes to social media I think it's important to remember this. If you run a luxury brand you might struggle with the advice in this book, or any of my books. The same can be said for brands who occupy the lower end of the market. That's not to say that I don't agree with those ends of the market. I'm more than happy to purchase products from a budget retailer to save a few pounds here and there. And I'm also more than happy to "splash the cash" at the right moment and opt for a more high end product. But when it comes to offering advice, my expertise lies in the mid-market.

If you are a business owner whose business occupies either the lower or the higher end of the market, don't be put off by this though. There will still be some truths that run through social media marketing which will apply to every end of the market.

Things like staying social and being consistent are things that are important no matter where you place your brand.

A Note on Social Media Managers

Whilst I have spoken about social media managers in previous books, I felt it was a topic worth covering again. Especially in the light of the increase in online market places which allow you to buy such services at a relatively low cost.

Market places such as Elance and oDesk have sprung up over recent years and whilst they are great for certain jobs (I even use them myself for transcribing audio for example), they can be dangerous to use for hiring social media managers.

That's not to say there aren't great social media marketers on these market places, it's just there are a lot of people who profess to be proficient in social media marketing where in fact they don't know enough.

The reason it's so important to get your social media manager right, is that they are taking control of your brand within a social field. You wouldn't outsource your customer relations in real life to somebody who didn't know about or didn't care about your business. It's a job that you need to take great time and care over choosing the right applicant. They need to be able to spell correctly every time and convey the tone of your brand correctly.

If you're a traditional British company with strong

British values and you employ an Australian social media marketer, you could find your brand weakening within social media.

Likewise, if you're an Australian brand, I might not be the best person to manage it for you. You'll notice how sometimes though you do need someone to manage your social media. I'm certainly not saying it's a bad thing. After all, I earn a living from managing other people's social media accounts. It's my profession.

I do however regularly turn down clients. Partly because I'm usually always fully booked and I try not to work with more than four clients at a time. That is partly because there is only so many hours in a day, but also because when I'm working with more than four brands, I begin to lose the tone or worse, the tones start to merge together with each brand.

I've also learnt in recent years that you can't manage a social media campaign for a brand in any less than 15 hours a week. 3 Hours a day, Monday to Friday gives me enough time to get my mind in place for the brand, come up with some engaging content and reply to the comments and messages that have been sent as we'll find out later in the book.

Engaging with your fans on social media networks, whether that's Google+, Facebook, Twitter or LinkedIn, is vital. If you don't engage, you won't succeed. All you will be doing is shouting a message that no one will want to hear.

So social media managers could be excellent for you. They can free up your time, which is invaluable if you're a small business or a startup with limited hours and limited resources. However, they don't come cheaply and you can't expect someone to manage your brand efficiently on social media in just a couple of hours a week.

It takes a lot of time, hard work and dedication to make social media work so you should expect to pay accordingly.

Social media managers can be great for your brand but they can also be very damaging.

Remember: Picking the wrong social media manager can have a negative effect on your brand and business.

Remember that social media marketing can work two ways. If you get it right, the sales can increase almost exponentially depending on your business type. But if you get it wrong, you could see sales drop if the person you bring in to manage your brand on social media doesn't know what they're doing, can't spell correctly and sends out messages which are inappropriate for your target audience, or just plain boring.

You could see your loyal customers leaving you for your competitors. It's not something you should stay up at night worrying about, it's just some food for thought. Choose your social media manager wisely.

GOOGLE+ AND SOCIAL MEDIA

Google+ doesn't sit by itself in the world of social media. There is Facebook, Twitter, Pinterest, LinkedIn, to name just the big players. As such, it's worth surveying what is out there and how Google's offering sits alongside the other options. In this section, we take a look at the history of Google, what Google+ is, whether or not social media on the whole is important, and whether or not Facebook or Google+ is best.

A Brief History of Google

Google, the world's largest search engine (by a very, very long way) is possibly the most important privatised organisation in the world today. The modern world runs on the Internet – for something that is so new in real terms it is immensely difficult to imagine life without the Internet. And it's almost as difficult to imagine the Internet without Google. In August 2012, the engine went down for just 4 minutes and the entire world's Internet traffic dropped by 40%. That's the kind of influence the web giant has – and it's only getting larger as the company continues to grow.

This section will explore the history of Google from the very beginning as a humble Ph.D. project right up to the giant that we all know and use today. This wouldn't be an easy section to write – a lot of research and fact-finding is needed. Fortunately, though, I've had a very special tool available to me. A tool that has in fact made the entire book possible. That tool, is the Google search engine.

The Early Days

Google started as a research Ph.D. project by Larry Page and Sergey Brin, both of whom are still very active within Google and together hold a 16% stake in Google's stock. Page and Brin are together number 13 and 14 on the Forbes 400 rich list, and first met at Stanford University, whilst they were both working in the computer science department. Page had begun to think about indexing web pages and Brin very shortly after joined him. Together they start working on their Ph.D. project that would eventually form Google.

Page and Brin's project, started in 1996, was originally known as BackRub, and was designed to find what websites link to a specific page. The rating of these "backlinks", as they're known, is still the fundamental pin in Google's searching algorithm, and is now called

"PageRank", after Larry Page. Anybody hoping to get to grips with running an Internet business and generating web traffic will always have PageRank as one of their top considerations – it is immensely important to get on the good side of Google if you want good web traffic. The simple truth is that just *so much* web traffic moves directly through Google's web servers – it holds a majority stake in the entire world of Internet users.

After developing BackRub, Page and Brin moved on with their idea and what was just a Ph.D. project had started to gain momentum – the domain google.com was registered on September 15th, 1997. Shortly after this they both abandoned the Ph.D. side of things and took Google to the next level – working towards turning the engine (which had already been proven a hit at Stanford) into a viable business.

The company itself had humble beginnings in a friend's garage about a year later. It should be remembered that even at this time the Internet was still a very 'young' technology – Page and Brin were lucky enough to be working right on the edge of the wave that would very quickly become a huge and multi-faceted part of modern society.

The Growth Of Google

Between 1998 and 2003, the company grew enormously quickly and soon dwarfed all of its rivals. Google is a wonderful example of the classic 'American Dream' company – it offered a better system than all of its competitors, quickly grew a vast user base, and attracted enormous investment at the same time from a multitude of companies. By June 1999, the company had attracted investment totalling $25 million, on the condition that the Google founders would take on a CEO to run the company as the investors, Sequoia Capital, were not comfortable with such a huge investment going into a company without the formal business structure they were used to.

Eric Schmidt was the first hire as CEO in 2001, and it's generally accepted that he, along with Page and Brin, steered Google in the right direction in business – allowing the company to grow responsibly and healthily. A difficult task bearing in mind the rate at which Google was gaining popularity among Internet users and advertisers alike.

A big change to Google's system came in 2000, when they started running text-based advertisements in their search results. This was the beginning of the monetisation of Google but at the start it didn't produce enough capital to support such a necessarily fast-growing business. As such, in 2003 Google announced a possible public offering of shares, and were shortly after approached by Microsoft to consider a merger. This deal never occurred (if it had, the technology landscape as we know it today would be enormously different) and Google went ahead with their IPO in 2004, raising $1.67 billion in capital, representing a market capitalisation of $23 billion. Within 7 years Page and Brin had built a company of the back of their Ph.D. project that could have bought the university it was started in!

The result of this enormous influx of capital and worth was simple – a huge proportion of Google's employees and other shareholders became millionaires overnight. Google – to put it simply – never had money troubles again, and was left to pursue other interests within the technology industry.

Further Growth and Expansion

Since 2004, Google has grown and grown into other areas, continued to adapt its search engine, and has been involved in an enormous amount of philanthropic activity. By this time, the user base had grown to make Google by far the most favoured search engine on the internet, and readily available text-based ads generated enough income to facilitate re-investment into other commercial interests.

In 2006, Google bought out the entire Mountain View complex (which it had previously only leased a few buildings in) in California and this has become the company's centre of operations, home to the famous and secret 'Google X' labs and the head office, alongside some of Google's servers and a lot more besides. The company also started acquisitions of many other technology companies and encompassing them under the Google banner, including the prominent blog website Blogger in 2003 and – in an enormous deal – YouTube in 2006 for $1.65 billion.

Google's success, they claim, is in part due to their business model and maxim, put simply: "don't be evil". This is their unofficial slogan and was detailed in their 2004 manifesto:

> *"Don't be evil. We believe strongly that in the long term, we will be better served — as shareholders and in all other ways — by a company that does good things for the world even if we forgo some short term gains."*

Google continued to grow up to the modern day, and has developed a host of new products and technology, such as the social networking site Google+, which, although failing to overtake Facebook, is still growing steadily as a social networking site. Other developments include the Google Drive system, which, along with GoogleDocs and Gmail, the company hopes will be used more and more in businesses and independent workers.

The company has worked – and is working on – a host of other projects and technologies. Google Earth was released in 2005 and has had huge success, beating its competitors hands down in true Google style. Microsoft and Apple – the two other technology giants in the western hemisphere – are the main competitors of Google but in many cases have been unable to get a foothold in Google's control of the market, particularly in web searching software – Microsoft's Bing engine has never lived up to the high hopes of its developers.

One of the largest 'fights' between the technology companies heated up in 2009. Known as the "Smartphone Wars", the struggle between Google, Apple and Microsoft to gain prominence in the mobile industry is still going on, though Google's Android system has again soared ahead of Apple's expensive iPhone and other competitors. The struggle broke out into a complex legal battle, with every company suing and countersuing every other company for various breaches of patents.

Google's web browser – Chrome – has also been a huge hit since being released in 2008, and was specifically designed to tie in with other Google products such as Gmail, Docs and Drive. In 2013 it held an estimated 39%

share in user ship, making it the world's most widely used web browser.

Another topic of much interest to technology companies in the last few years has been Google's collaborations with various companies, including work with NASA in data-management systems and other subjects of mutual interest, including working towards an entrepreneurial space industry. Google has also announced partnerships with AOL, NewsCorp and Sky, and, most interestingly, has even signed a deal allowing The Pope to have his own channel on YouTube.

Don't Be Evil

Google's huge financial success has allowed its creators to follow through with their unofficial motto and start a philanthropic campaign. Both Page and Brin have announced on numerous occasions that they intend to help solve the world's problems with technology, and Google's financial status means it is more that capable of hiring the best people for the job at hand. Google's philanthropic wing, google.org, was started in 2005 with a grant of $1 billion, and has worked on various projects, including work into a high-functioning plug-in hybrid-electric vehicle. Other projects the charitable arm is focussing on is work towards renewable energy that can be cheaper that coal, and information-based charitable work such as Google Crisis Response (used to locate missing people and map a crisis situation) and Google Flu – used to track disease trends in the developing world.

Alongside philanthropic technological research, Google has continued to design products for its richer customers.

The top-secret labs at Google X, although labelled by some as at least in part a popularity campaign, has started to churn out some interesting designs such as a self-driving car (Google has predicted that they will be available to the public in 5 years) and the impressive Google Glass – a wearable computer operated by voice recognition. These pet projects, along with many others, are expected to grow in popularity as the years go on.

Page and Brin are both private investors in a wide variety of philanthropic research towards "solving really big problems through technology". One that grabbed the world's imagination in 2013, for example, was a Dutch project to create a 'test-tube' hamburger. The project, backed anonymously by Brin until the results were out, was a success – and although it may be a long time till everybody catches onto the idea of a burger grown in a lab, the fact is these burgers *could* be made sustainably in the future.

Google enjoys its lab's top-secret and mysterious reputation, and cultivates it by not letting the public – or its competitors – know everything that's occurring behind closed doors. The same applies for a lot of Google's projects outside the lab, and this has worked in its favour – every new release from the company is followed by media attention and often studied obsessively by bloggers and technology reporters. Put simply, mystery has worked for Google.

The Future

The future of Google looks much like it's a past – a continual rise as a technology company with long-term interests and generally responsible behaviour. Google has not been without controversy over the years – they are being investigated for tax avoidance in the UK, and it has been involved in a fair few patent battles – but they look set to continue growing into new areas of the technology industry and develop their old systems.

There is a constant fear in modern society that some companies are too large to be sustainable and 'safe' for the consumer – Google has been accused many times of monopolising industries, and it is a truly vast company with 70 offices in 40 different countries. Even the word "google" has become a verb, meaning "to search something on the internet".

So, it is understandable that some people are concerned about the future when one private company is so influential in the modern world and looks set to be more so as time goes on. But if there is going to be a private company that has significant influence on the public, at least it's one who's motto is "don't be evil", is known for its charitable side, and works towards technological solutions to the world's problems. Putting it simply, things could be far worse.

What is Google+?

At its very simplest explanation, because I personally think Google+ can get a little complicated if you're not used to it, it's a really effective way to share content amongst the existing Google platforms, and it identifies contacts based on what you share, creating separate groups. It's a personal service, identify things for you, and you alone. That still sounds quite complicated doesn't it? Put simply, it's a lot more forward-thinking, and a lot more efficient than Facebook, with more scope for search integration, purely because it has the world's biggest search engine behind it.

Google+ is a social networking site launched by Google in 2011. Google+ allows you to build an extensive profile and share information with other people. It combines the features of several popular social media sites, such as Twitter and Facebook, to provide the best user experience. Another good thing about Google+ is that it allows you to protect your privacy and control who can see the information you share.

It has a variety of features, such as Circles, letting you organise your contacts into separate and bespoke groups, Stream, keeping you up to date on activities from your circles as above, Sparks, feeding you content based on your personal interests, and Hangouts, a group video chat app. These all help push Google+ in front of Facebook with its simple chat, and 'Like' functions. So that is the basic summary, but as this book is all about Google+, we'll now dive into a bit more detail.

Google+ Profiles

It's important to keep in mind that any Google+ account is based on a Google profile. Therefore, a working Google account is needed for Google+. The profiles were actually the first step into expanding user accounts on the network.

A profile connected to your Google+ page allows you

to share certain bits of information with the world. You can share personal details such as your name, birthday, location or phone number. You can fully control which details are visible to the world, and you can always restrict certain bits of information if you choose so. A profile allows you to build a short personal bio, share selected info and add links to your web sites.

Also, Google doesn't require to share much information unless you want. You can build the whole profile using only your name and you will never be forced to share anything else.

The best thing about Google+ profile is that you can fully control the audience and restrict the information as you see fit. There will often be some info you might want to share with your friends but not your co-workers. Or something you want only your family to see. Google makes it easy to restrict this info to target audience quickly and easily. This is where Google Circles come in handy.

Google+ Circles

Google+ uses a very effective concept of "circles". A circle is simply a collection of people with whom you wish to connect. Each Google+ account includes three pre-defined circles: friends, family and acquaintances. Of course, you may create your own, customized circles (such as co-workers, online friends, and more). You choose how to categorize people in a way that's the most convenient for you. Also, remember that you can put the same person into more than one circle, if you feel like this categorization works the best.

One important thing to note about Circles: putting

someone in your circle means that you choose to follow this person. However, it doesn't necessarily mean that a person follows you back. Circles can work as a one-way relationship, so you can make separate circles for companies and other profiles you wish to follow but you don't expect them to follow back.

The best thing about Google+ Circles is that they allow you to share information with a specific group (circle) and not the others. This way, you can read the content from the selected groups and not the others.

It also works the other way around. You can always restrict the information you wish to share only with people in a certain circle and not with others. Sharing always comes with multiple levels of privacy, so you can customize these settings as much as you want.

For example, you may choose to share your address and phone number only with people in your family or friends circle. Using a handy interface and with only a few clicks, you can restrict this information (address and phone number) to everyone else. This way, you can protect your privacy while keeping an open and vivid Google+ profile.

Is Social Media Important?

Social Media Marketing cannot be understated. Its roll in online business is increasing year on year and my prediction is that this will continue to rise in the forthcoming years. While search engine optimization has been on the lips of every marketer for the past ten years, I feel the next ten years will be the years of social.

I've previously written two books on social media marketing: "Facebook Business Basics" and "Twitter Business Basics". Each addressed the two biggest social networks respectively. They have helped thousands of small business owners and entrepreneurs take their business into the social realm.

So why bother with another social network – why bother with Google?

Is it because Google+ links to your YouTube account? Is it because Google+ has Hangouts? Is it because search engine results are becoming influenced by social links? Well actually it's all of this as we'll come to see later on in the book.

One of the biggest differences between Google+ and Facebook that I'd like to touch on at this point is that when you're logged into your Google account, anyone that's in your circles can recommend links on a Google search results page. If one of my friends have recently read and +1'd an article about the latest iPhone and I search for iPhone reviews, that article may well show up higher than others. That's not because the article is any better, or because it has more links, or because it's longer or because it's been optimised more efficiently, it's purely because my friend liked it. My friend +1'd it which means that I may be more prone to liking it. Of course, Google isn't stupid, if you repeatedly don't click on a link as recommended by one of your friends on Google+, it will reduce the frequency that it shows you such links. However, the more you click on links that have been +1'd by your friends, the more those friends will influence your search engine results page.

What Google have done is to bring social accreditation

right into search engine results pages. Unlike Facebook, which works in a closed ecosystem, and Twitter which isn't that engrained to other platforms, Google+ is integrating its social aspect which is growing with its massive search presence.

Whilst there is certainly a school of thought that suggests you should be everywhere, and I tend to agree that that's the right move to make if possible, it's also important to state at this early stage that if you're already on Facebook, Twitter, Pinterest or LinkedIn, you've got a strategy and it's already taking up too much time, adding another social network into the frame is not a good move. Some businesses work better on certain social networks. Cupcake businesses for example, work very well on Pinterest, but you might find a business advisor is more suited to LinkedIn. These are generalisations though and there's no reason why a business advisor couldn't rock it on Pinterest and a cupcake maker couldn't be awesome on LinkedIn. It's all about finding out what works for you and what works for your business. There really is no right or wrong answer. The only right thing to do is to make sure whatever you do, you do well. If that means only taking up the reins on one social network at a time, that's fine. Don't over stretch yourself because all you'll do is diminish any effect that your efforts will have.

If you're a one-man-band, like many small businesses are, or if you're just starting out, remember that you don't have to be on every social network. Pick one, maybe two and do it well. With that being said, if you do have more resources (money or time), being on more than one social network is a massive advantage. Why? Well, different social networks attract different groups of people.

Twitter has a relatively young crowd whereas Pinterest is made up by predominately female users. What this means is your business can reach different groups of people. Whilst this might not apply to every business I do feel that the more people you can reach the higher your chances of success with social media marketing.

I worked with a plumber who had a good presence on Facebook but was unsure about whether any other networks were applicable to him. After only a short period, he was rocking it on Twitter as well. But then he came back to me and asked whether there'd be any point going for Pinterest.

After sitting down and sorting out strategy we realized there was a missive gap in the market. Whilst the users are predominately female, and the pins generally tend to revolve around cupcakes, nice interiors and cute cats, with a few clever images (some of which were rather tenuously linked) he really enhanced his presence online and reached a whole new group of people: female users aged between 20 and 35.

Female users aged between 20 and 35 still need a plumber every now and again and who would they go to? The Yellow pages? AAA Plumbing? Or to the plumber that they've built up a relationship with on Pinterest already? They go back to him.

This is one example of how businesses that you may have thought to be irrelevant to certain social networks can in fact work very well. If none of your competitors are using it that might be a sign that it's not worth doing, however I like to think of it as an open opportunity. If none of your competitors are using it – that market's yours. Go out and grab them and make the most of them.

Facebook vs Google+

There is an argument brewing. You might not be too aware of it, because you won't hear it on the street or in your every day working life, but online, this is a debate that rages.

Do you use Facebook, whether it be for business of pleasure? I'm guessing you do, because at last count the online community was hitting the 1 billion active users per month. Lofty heights, and that figure will only rise. I'm quite the Facebook addict if I'm honest. Most of my clients employ me for my Facebook marketing skills. I wrote my first ever book on Facebook marketing.

Do you use Twitter? The favourite go-to of celebs the world over, tweeting their opinions and rogue thoughts for fans to hear, follow and re-tweet. It's popularity speaks for itself, and again, the number of regular users grows and grows. I highlighted the real benefits in my previous book, *Twitter Business Basics,* so I won't repeat them all here. In brief, I'd say it's a great way to reach out to people you don't know, with a few hundred words' characters.

If we're saying these two social networking giants are the main big-hitters, then the raging online debate asks whether Google+ will take over the mantle and become the king of the social networking world.

Some say yes, some say no, some just don't know. For now, it's a matter of opinion, but there are several factors that mean that yes, it's quite the possibility.

After the last section, we're all up to speed with what

Google is; basically the king of all search engines, and the one we all generally use when we're trying to find something. It is also a seriously money-spinning big business, built up from the very roots into the giant it is today. Google+ was launched in September 2011, and at first glance, nobody really thought much of it. When compared with Facebook's all singing, all dancing 'Like' button, and its ability to share, and in some cases, over-share, every detail of its users' lives, Google+ wasn't really much different, and it struggled because of it. However, fast forward a couple of years and with a few clever marketing ploys, Google+ had racked up user figures of around 300 million users monthly. That's a big jump, and it now threatens Facebook and Twitter's crowns on traffic and fancy apps alone.

Basically, Google is using its money and name to push ahead. Also, add in the fact that to use various other Google programmes, such as Gmail, you have to sign up for a Google+ account - a sneaky, yet effective way to gain users. Some find this a rather forceful tactic, but there's no denying that it works.

As for its name, Google has a lot of power in business, and companies and advertisers are quite happy to invest, whereas they're not so quick to throw money into Facebook, with previous advertising having not produced such amazing results for business.

Shrewd business use and a lot of research, based on watching how Facebook and Twitter have worked before it, means Google+ has picked up and righted the wrongs the former two made. This, twinned with the fact that the search element really comes to the fore with this new social networking giant, means Google+ has a lot going for it. Because of Facebook's ongoing dramas with privacy settings, it often means that posts don't appear in Google search results, however anything posted on Google+ will, which is an undeniable advantage in business, which is going more and more down the social networking route.

Should Facebook and Twitter be quaking in their cyber-boots? Whilst none of us can predict the future reliably, it's quite likely that Google as a business will push its social networking gem further into the fore, meaning Facebook and Twitter will need to up the ante if they're wanting to stay firmly on top.

Whilst Google+ does seem a little confusing to regular users of Facebook, there's no denying that it's a much more polished, efficient machine, and for promotional use, it could win hands down. Business will always win through in the end, as we know.

For now, the three major players in the social networking world can co-exist quite harmoniously, but one thing's for sure, the current big two shouldn't rest on their laurels if they want to stay top-dog. Based on how things are now, if things stay static with them, then Google+ will run through and pip them to the post.

Google are constantly trying to link their products together in a more efficient manner. You can see this through the linking of comments on YouTube videos and Google+ accounts. The reviews on Google+ local pages, also appear on Google Maps. And endorsements from Google+ pages are beginning to appear in search engine results pages.

What this means is for the small business who relies on Google so heavily to be found online, ignoring one of their products can be almost as damaging as ignoring all of them.

That's not to say that you need to be on YouTube, Google+ and embracing Google friendly search engine optimization. Especially around local. It does however mean that you need to be aware of how the products link together and why that matters to you and your business.

Ignoring it isn't really an option any more. Google aren't going to unlink their products. The links are only going to be embedded deeper and deeper. In the future you may see comments left on an article from a post on Google+ appearing in the search engine results pages. So when you search for "fence panels", you might see a review from your friend of "fence panels".

Google are already using Google+ profile pictures controversially in adverts. Data is what drives Google and if they can find another way to link two pieces of data together to enhance the user experience or increase revenue my guess is, they will.

Whilst their mantra is "Don't be evil" that mantra will only survive if they're making money.

I still remember the time when Google+ just launched and some of the social media "experts" believed that it is the "killer" of Facebook era. But nothing happened at all. Facebook still dominates the Social Media Platforms beyond reasonable doubt. So, there is no as such comparison we can make among Facebook and Google+. It is the reality that Facebook has about 55% domination upon all the social media platforms whereas Google+ has only 2%. That is why some people describe Google+ as a 'Ghost Town'. And when it comes to **consumer log in,** Facebook has about 62% login percentile. Whereas, Google+ has just 18%.

Interface Differences

Since the day of launch back in 2011, Google+ has been through many interfaces. There are number of changes on almost monthly basis Google indulge into their social media platform. When it comes to Facebook, the major change in interface was the conversion of Wall to Timeline. The colour of the interface is still the same though. Otherwise on quarterly basis, very minor changes are made by the development team. Since the day it started back in 2004, Facebook has changed and it is most certainly not the same as it was ten years ago. So there is quite balance in that comparison.

Profile & Chat

Google+ has more features to edit when it comes to building a profile than Facebook. You can edit individual tabs and a number of things on Google+. You can add the links to your websites and other profiles on Google+, whilst on Facebook, you can add your website only to your profile but you are not allowed to add the links to your other social media profiles. The chat facility at both Google+ and Facebook is pretty much same; you can add people to conversation, send and receive pictures and other multimedia through chat. But on Google+, there is something quite unique and different, which is known as Google+ Hangouts. Hangouts allows you to add up to 9 people in a conversation and can live broadcast yourself. You can even record a live broadcast session through it for viewing it later on.

Comparison Between Both Networks as Marketing Platforms

There are quite a few decent features and a very BIG audience on Facebook is available. And this is what any marketer/business needs right? The more people to reach out and the better way to market their services or product. Facebook pages, groups, profiles, video sharing facility, adding pictures along with the post, posting questions, creating polls, generating likes, sharing other links on Facebook (to your blogs or website), adding the cover photo which can represent your Business… it pretty much everything.

But when it comes to Google+, there are also some features which are very good. Like on Facebook, Google+ has profiles, pages, communities and other features but what makes it different and unique is the Hangouts, Authorship Markups on the profile to your website, circles, "what's hot", local places ratings. Google+ also has a decent audience.

SETTING UP YOUR GOOGLE+ ACCOUNT

What are Google+ Circles?

One of the greatest features is called "Circles". Google+ Circles is the feature, which allows users to create groups within their buddy lists. This feature helps the users to share the relevant information or content with the desired group of people. At the same time, it allows you to see the posts made by "Specific Circle" right away.

You can assign a specific name to any circle. No one within a circle can see the name and other people within the circle. It works more like the "real life circles", the circles that are intangible and we all create in our minds.

You can create various circles according to:

- Close Friends
- College Mates
- Co-Workers
- People we look up to
- Prospects/Customers

And so on…

Don't mix up Circles with Google Groups

I've seen some people saying that Circles is the newer version of Google Groups. I completely disagree, because Circles work very different than the Groups. There are three key features that make Circles way different than the Google Groups.

- In Google Groups, all members know the name of that specific group.
- All members are aware of the purpose of group
- Everyone can see the other members within the group

It will be a more accurate comparison of circles, if you compare the circles with a "twitter private list" or the "Facebook friends list". Because people within a Circle is the compilation of people at your own end. That is why people within a list/circle have no idea about the name that you have given to the circle or the purpose of yours that why you made this circle.

Greater Freedom to Privacy

If you want to share the post within the specific group of people/Circle. On the top right corner of the post, you will see a small tab called "limited". By clicking on that, you will be able to see the number of people who can see the post. You can even share the post with multiple circles or even with the combination of circles and individuals. Like I've mentioned earlier that you can control the visibility of your post to the specific circle. It is the great feature similar to other platforms like Face book , Twitter etc. For example, if you have a circle of prospects, you can share the blogs and latest happenings within your business with your prospect which is the concerned audience to that content. Similarly if you want to share a video of your pet with your friends, you can share it with the specific circle of your close friends while your prospects could not be able to see the post of that video. Even you can control that who can comment on the post.

You can even Change the Order of your Circles

You can arrange/re-arrange the order of your circles by simply "drag and drop". So if you want to see the posts on the top by your friends/family, simply drag the circle and drop it on the top and similar you can arrange the other circles.

Final Thoughts

Google+ works much like the other social networking platforms. But there are some great features which are available at Google+ and make it way different than other platforms. Google+ can help you out to think out of the box and create and integrate your marketing by going out and getting more audience. The feature of "Circles" can help you a lot to create the lists of prospects. So that you can reach out your audience to share you specific activities with them and can see their happenings as well.

Making Your Google+ Page Look Great

Making your page look good on Google+ is really quite important to a successful Google+ marketing campaign. It's your brand on one of the biggest social networks, so you really should be caring about it. If you're a plumber you wouldn't let your firm drive around in vans where your logos on a slant. If you're a cake decorator you wouldn't put and advert in the local yellow pages with a spelling mistake. It's these kind of things that you need to be checking, double checking and triple checking on Google+ because after all if your pages looks rubbish, it looks like you don't care. It looks like your brand doesn't care. Attention to detail therefore is paramount. Keeping it simple and basic like I've tried to throughout the book, what I'm going to do it go down the Google+ page and point out the areas you should be paying special attention to in order to make your page look great.

GOOGLE+ BUSINESS BASICS

The first thing you'll see at the top of your Google+ page is a massive cover photo. This when you scroll all the way up takes up the whole screen on many computer displays. For me therefore this is really important to get right. You need to select an image or photo that represents your brand well and whilst there are some exceptions I believe that stock photos can never do that effectively. Invest in some decent photography of your shop, maybe of your staff, maybe of your work. Whilst this might cost a little bit in the short run, the long-term benefits of this I think are worth it. Imagine going back to the example of the plumber, his staff of ten stood outside the company offices with the sign written brands on either side polished and shiny looking. What does that say? This says this is a well-organised company that is professional, clean and tidy and aren't going to mess me about. It says this is a plumbing company that I want to deal with. What about a florist, or how about a picture of your shop on a busy Saturday afternoon. If you hire a half decent photographer he'll be able to give you some insights into nice angles and compositions; but imagine if you will that image of your shop on a busy Saturday afternoon with a really, really slow shutter speed with hundreds of people whizzing past it, and blurring the picture. Your shop stands proud against the backdrop of rushing shoppers. What does this say? To me it could say that your shop is a pillar amongst the local community, standing still and staying there whilst the rest of society moves by. You could also think more simply perhaps that this is a florist with a shop. It might sound obvious but there are many florists out there that don't have shops, they work from home and whilst there's nothing wrong with that if you do have a shop as a florist perhaps you'd want to sing about it. You want to say that you are a respected shop in your local area; you're not just operating out of a garage. It might be that photography isn't what you require, in which case I would strongly suggest hiring a graphic designer to give you an image that you can use for your cover image that is striking and looks great. The last thing you want is pixelated, poor quality images.

Moving down, though sticking with the graphic designer theme, you'll notice the profile picture. On Facebook, Twitter and LinkedIn these are all square but on Google+ its circular. This can cause some problems if you're just planning to take your profile picture from one of the other social networks and upload it to Google+.

Quite often you'll cut off the corners of your logo. Again, this looks like you don't care. If you're not too confident in photo shop, get on that phone to the graphic designer again or maybe you've got a nephew or a niece who's a bit savvy with photo shop. You can always e-mail me as well. My e-mail address is at the end of the book and I'm always happy to help out my readers.

A little bit further down, you'll see a number of tabs and clicking on them brings up a number of different pieces of information:

- Your posts.
- Your images.
- Your information as a brand.

For me this section is really simple. You click the edit button and you fill in every box available to you. Social networks are pretty good at making their pages look great. All you need to do is fill in the blanks. There's nothing worse with a space where there should be a map. Make sure you input the details carefully and you'll be sure to have a great looking Google+ page in no time.

I've included a link to a cheat sheet at the end of the book and I've posted the graphic in as well. For me this is really handy to give to your designer, it gives them all the required information for image sizes and it helps you to visualise what your page will look like when you've filled it up. Getting the right image sizes from your graphic designer is really, really important because having distorted images, whether they're cropped wrong, pixelated or blurry just doesn't look good. Make sure you care enough about your brand to make it look as good as it does in the real world.

Enabling Authorship

Google Authorship is a feature which enables you to link your published content on any specific domain with your Google+ Profile. Note that Authorship will only work on a Google+ Profile at the time of writing, and not a page. However, you can enable Publisher rights instead. More on that later.

Google announced in 2013 that they now support authorship mark-up for Google+ which means authors can connect their content on Google+ from all around the internet.

Authorship is indeed a pretty awesome way to provide writers and authors more visibility during search results. And at the same time, it assigns a face to the one who is looking at results. It is a great way to market yourself and attract more clients if you are only relying on your website.

Here is how it looks on a Google search results page:

> Inside Google+ — How the Search Giant Plans to Go :
> www.wired.com/epicenter/2011/06/inside-google-plus.../1
>
> by Steven Levy · in 838,229 Google+ circles · More by S
> Jun 28, 2011 – Follow **@stevenlevy**. **Google**, the world's company, is formally making its pitch to become a major networking.

So in order to set this up, you'll want to head over to the Authorship signup page (https://plus.google.com/authorship). You'll also need to make sure you have a profile photo with a recognisable headshot and make sure a by-line containing your name appears on each page of your content (for example, "By

Steven Levy"). Make sure your byline name matches the name on your Google+ profile. Don't go using fluffypony96 on your blog and Claire James on your Google+ profile. Finally, you'll need to verify you have an email address (such as stevenlevy@wired.com) on the same domain as your content. There is a way around that if you don't have an email address on the same domain, but I'll leave it to Google to explain that one.

<u>Organize You Google+ Profile</u>

Google use the image for your Authorship direct from your Google+ Profile. Which means you are required to create your own Google+ account. Of course, you should probably have one of those already by this point in the book.

Once you are done with creating your profile, you need to upload a photo to your profile image, which should look good in full size or even in thumbnail. After that fill out the information like the occupation you have, education and it will help people to recognize you.

After that, it is more important to add the complete URL and name of your Blog/Website. In the section called "Contributor to". Next step is to click the edit button then scroll down to the Contributor Section, and add the custom link and fill out the URL and label fields. Make sure, you are specifying the name of your homepage.

When you're done, just hit the Save button and then click on Done edit at the top of the page. Make sure by double checking the contributor section.

<u>Configure rel="author" for Other Blogs</u>

Once you are done with proper configuration for your Google+ profile, you need to set up rel="author" on single-author blogs.

You will be required to create a link to your Google+ Profile of yours if you have done work over other pages or blogs where your writer material is published. You need to creak a link which include rel="author" attribute to your Google+ Profile.

Google+ Publisher

Enabling Google+ Publisher status will allow your brand to sit in the Google Knowledge Graph (providing Google thinks you're worthy). Here's how it looks on Google:

In order to connect this up, you'll need to add in a line of code or two. If you're uncomfortable doing this, just have a word with a competent web developer, or drop me an email. In short, here is the code you'll require:

```
<a href="https://plus.google.com/123456789123456789" rel="publisher">
```

Connecting Your YouTube Account

Google+ has a new strategy to make your social media presence consistent by having a single identity across all over your social media profiles. And that's the reason why they are testing some beta feature of linking your YouTube channel up with your Google+ Profile Page.

This is indeed a great news for those who have a very decent number of followers on their YouTube channel, and are looking forward to make their YouTube Channel more successful with the help of a Google+ Profile. At the same time, it is a great news for those who already have their Google+ Profile and want to market their services or products more with the help of a YouTube Channel.

Let's take a look how it actually works.

How to Link up YouTube Channel with Google+ by opt into the Beta Test

Make sure that any Google account you have is already associated with your YouTube channel and it has its own Google+ account as well. If you want to set up a new profile for Google+, then go to the website http://plus.google.com and follow the instructions to create a new profile.

If you already have a Google+ profile and want to

connect to your YouTube channel, all you need to do is add your Google account as an associated account with your YouTube channel as manager for the page.

Once you are done with setting up the Google+ and YouTube profiles, the next step is to connect your Google+ page (which is a BETA version as of writing). You will find it under **advanced account settings.**

Then select one of the three given options, and after you're done with that, you can tap into the Google+ community as BETA tester to share the experience of yours.

Advantages of Linking up Google+ with YouTube

You can have the access to many different features by connecting your Google+ profile with YouTube. You can add tools such as multiple managers for your channel, you can give a name or edit the existing name of your YouTube channel the same way as your brand page on Google+. Which means a greater flexibility. And you can even make that name consistent with your profile at Google+. The other perks you can have are like YouTube tab on your Page, you can easily broadcast from Hangouts the same stream of your YouTube plus seamless capabilities of video sharing.

The duration period of this BETA testing service is about 14 days. Which means that you have the choice to participate and can choose to unlink the both accounts of yours within that duration. If you do not unlink the account within that time, the changes will remain constant and it cannot be undone.

The facility or feature of cross linking within 2 different

social media tools is just a beginning of the whole change I feel Google will be implementing over forthcoming years. Why? Well having accounts linked allows you to market your business through the same account on different channels. Good for business. Good for the web.

You can also join the discussion upon this BETA service over Google+ Community and can even share the experience and the results with others who are looking or planning to integrate their YouTube channel with Google+.

ENGAGING ON GOOGLE+

Engaging with your followers on Google+ is vital. I've previously stated that it's better to have 100 fans that are engaged, than 100,000 that aren't. This is certainly true on Google+.

What is the point of having thousands of fans who don't engage with you. They don't talk to you, they don't +1 any posts, they don't click on any links, they don't acknowledge any photos and they don't watch any of your videos. You're pushing content out into a black hole. Nobody is reading it and it's having no effect on your business. You need to engage your fans from the beginning as with any social media network. Facebook, Twitter, Google+, LinkedIn, they all revolve around engagement and enhancing your engagement should be the number one thing on your to-do-list. The following chapter goes over this concept in more detail, but remember to keep engagement at the front of your mind as we whizz through this chapter.

Creating a Strategy for your Google+ Campaign

This following section is lifted almost verbatim from my book, *Twitter Business Basics*. The reason for this is simple, it was well received and applies equally to Google+. So often I hear social media marketers, in fact marketers in general, over emphasizing campaign strategies when in reality, the best ones are usually the simple ones. Of course, you can add fairy dust over the top and dress the following up all you like, but my opinion is that a strategy should be kept simple and easy to follow. That way, you know when you're going off topic. Anyway, that's why I've decded to reuse this section. For those of you who have read my previous book, I'm sure you understand.

Social media marketing plans seem to be the holy grail for many small businesses. Spurred on by the pretentious preaching's of 'lifestyle coaches', it's easy to get suckered into the belief that there is a single PDF document that will answer all your questions, tell you what to tweet, and perhaps even do it for you. Then, this magical document will increase your sales overnight and you will be able to retire and 'live the good life'. Life doesn't work like that. With this in mind, here is my Google+ marketing plan blueprint. It will not answer all your questions or tell you what to tweet, and it will certainly not do it for you.

For me, a social media marketing plan is a document that outlines your strategy. It sounds simple, but many choose to complicate this simple definition by suggesting the inclusion of a timetable or other silly things. It's also worth remembering that your marketing plan will be different to your competitors, or to your friend's business's social strategy. To get started with your own Google+ plan, I suggest going back to those questions I posed at the beginning. Why Google+? What do you want from it? This way, you can go into battle with a plan rather than blindly posting away. Posting without a plan like this won't get you very far. Instead, decide what you want, and how you will get it. Now, for the holy grail. On the following page, you will see a series of sentences, ready to be completed by, you guessed it, *you!* This will form the basis for your Google+ marketing plan. It's not a concrete formula, as things change, and you'll possibly want to add in a sentence here or there, but on the whole, this document will become your Google+ marketing plan. Tear it out (or copy it if you're reading it on the Kindle) and pin it up on your wall above your computer. I know you could just define everything in your head, but having it printed out in front of you in your line of sight makes it impossible to forget. Now, without further ado, drumroll please…

MY GOOGLE+ MARKETING PLAN

I will use Google+ to...

I will achieve this by...

I will measure my success through...

I will review this marketing plan on...

That is it. It's not complicated, there are no hidden questions, just a simple set of statements that will be unique to you and will help you to set goals, measure them, and meet them on Google+.

Driving Traffic to your Google+ Page

When it comes to driving traffic to your Google+ page, it can often be difficult to think where to start. It needn't be though; the best ways of driving the traffic to your Google+ page are always the simplest. If you send out emails to people put a link to your Google+ page in the signature. That way every time you send an email to somebody they see that you've got a Google+ page. You could maybe print it on your receipts that you give your customers or maybe you add it to your order confirmation that every customer receives when they place an order on your website. These are the obvious places to put it and this is what drives the most traffic, however it would be a bit unfair of me to just state that and say it's up to you because no doubt after a while you'll be wondering why isn't working. This is a common mistake small business owner's make. Placing a link to their social media accounts on emails and receipts and just expecting it to work. Unfortunately it's not quite that simple. Think of it as a call to action, you need to give the customer a reason to visit your page. I'm not necessarily talking about giving them 10% off when they circle you on Google+ or like you Facebook or follow you on Twitter. What I'm talking about is asking them a question, asking them to go onto their social media and engage with you. You've probably seen the signs on posters all across the country, on TV adverts and even on radio adverts saying like us on Facebook. The one word I'd say is, why? Why would the customer want to like you on Facebook or circle you on Google+? You haven't told them why they should. Give them a reason; ask them something. One of my favourite fish and chips shops near me got on their boxes- let us know what you thought on Facebook. They're not directly asking for a like but by god do they get some. They're asking the customer a question, they're asking them to directly engage with them and they're doing it in such a way that suggests that there might be a person at the other end of that computer who wants to know what there meal was like. When it comes to driving traffic to your Google+ page, you need to be thinking along the same lines. Sure, place links in prominent places such as email signatures, and yes, on the receipts or packaging that you use if you could get them printed so it says circle us on Google+, that's great. However, take it a step further and ask them to engage with you at that point. Make it sound like you're a human at the other end, after all you are. It's something so simple, but no one's doing it. Start now and you could really see the benefits later.

Using Google+ Hangouts

Are you looking to add some flashy video to your Social Media Marketing? With the help of Google+ Hangouts, you can make it happen relatively easily. By using Google+ Hangouts, you can perform multiple tasks at the same time e.g.:

- You can use the video chat with up to 9 people instantly.
- You can share files and documents.
- You can chat alongside while watching a video over YouTube together.
- You can share your screen with others.
- You can even record live chat session for viewing it later.
- You can even broadcast your live chat to anyone.

New to Google+ Hangouts?

Google+ Hangouts is simple and easy to use and, of course, is free. All you need to do is to create a Google+ account and then click the button says "Start Hangout". It's that simple. All you need to do is to click on the green button and then decide whom you want to invite.

Get Ready to Be Creative!

I have personally figured out four very basic and creative ways to use Hangouts for bringing in more business that I have utilised with clients.

1. Start Working by Collaborations (Crowdsourcing)

Google+ Hangouts is an ideal place where you can share the ideas of yours for new or existing products, services and even can offer solutions to you audience.

It is a place where you can provide valuable advice and expertise to your prospects. And because the content often spreads, it will help to convert the prospects into actual customers.

2. Questions/Answer Sessions

Asking questions can help you out a lot in order to improve the quality of your services/product. You can collect very valuable information from your customers through Q/A sessions, which means it will help you to improve the experience of your customers and business as well.

3. Create A Workshop or Demonstration

One of the best and easiest way to give value to the customers while endorsing your business is to create a demonstration or workshop. It is the best practice for the businesses who are more viable at one-on-one demonstrations. Workshops can help you to convince your audience in order to convert them into actual customers. You can provide the audience with your contact information too and encourage their questions at a later date too. If you're in their phone as the person to call when they need advice on something, you're on to a winner! They'll be converting into a paying customer sooner rather than later!

4. More Giveaways, Meaning More Customers

It is the best practice, especially at the end of every year when your store room is stacked up with last season's products. It will drive a huge amount of traffic to your Google+ page which means enhanced exposure and perhaps a few more sales. People who will test your service or product will recognise the value of that product and become a customer. Of course, you need to engage your fans and make sure that you are providing your audience the product or service that can help them and not just a rubbish product at a discounted price.

Google+ Communities

One of the coolest feature of Google+ is Google+ Communities. It's indeed a great opportunity for the people who want to market their brand or product because Google+ Communities allows you to network, build and engage their businesses.

<u>What is a Google+ Community?</u>

It is a place to engage and meet the people who shares the same interest as you do. if you were facing any problems in engaging the audience in the past, then probably it's the best time to take a 'second look' over the topics and active communities that you might be interested in.

You can create communities which could be Public or Private, putting discussion over almost every possible topic to this is the right time to jump in and market yourself in a better way.

How a Google+ Community Can Benefit Your Business

In almost every single aspect you can think of, Google+ Community can benefit a business of yours. All you need to do is to consider some reasons for joining the Communities at Google+

You can grow you network by the help of sharing your expertise and knowledge with the community who shares the same interest of yours. You can easily find the people who are passionate about the topic that matches yours. You can answer the questions by people and can share your thoughts.

With help of Google+ Communities, you can make a well focused group for the business of yours. So make sure while joining community/communities that you have to get some good impact for your business through listening to the discussion. If you got a question to ask, yes you should go ahead and ask the question, make your contribution in different discussions.

You can discover many new ideas through discussions for your blog articles or even get the better idea to make your services or the products of your business better.

You can start your own discussions as communities allow you to do so. it means that you can post an article or might share something that can grab the attention of your target audience.

You can even drive the traffic to your website by engaging the other people from the communities. As it is one of the best opportunity to post and article or probably for sharing some content from your website.

Tips & Thing That You Should Consider

Here are some tips (if you're going ahead) to find the communities that suites your Business:

- You can search or reach your target market with the help of Searching them by Topics.
- You can even use the Keywords which are useful for your business.
- With the help of searching the competitors of your business.

If you want to start your own Google+ Community it's even better. It's really easy and take less than 5 minutes but make sure one thing, you are going to put some useful content in the community. Though it takes some time to seed anything with beneficial content. But after some time, you will definitely get there.

- First of all, add few lines in the About section.
- Then assign by going into the tab of settings, your can add multiple owners and moderators.
- You can add different topics which can be seen right in the side bar, then seed these topics with quality content.
- You can even made some rules for your community.
- Then you can even edit the Privacy if your don't want to make it a Public Community.

In conclusion, the reason why you should embrace Google+ Communities is just to make your marketing strategy more viable and to reach a wider audience and connect people and make them believe that YOU hold the key to their solutions. Of course, you do actually need to spread that answer, holding without sharing isn't very nice now, is it?

GOOGLE ADVERTISING

Advertising is the one word that scares all small business owners it seems. The more I talk to people, the more I realize that they're scared of advertising, especially online. They either think it's going to cost thousands of pounds or it won't produce any results. Of course that is possible. You can spend thousands of pounds on advertising and yes, if done badly it might not produce results. However, done well, advertising online can be extremely lucrative.

I'm going to keep this section short and sweet, as advertising within Google+ hasn't really began yet in the same way it has on Facebook. Rest assured, I'll be keeping my eye out though, and as and when I deem necessary, there will be an updated version of this book available!

AdWords is perhaps the most well-known online advertising platform. It allows you to place adverts on the Google search networks. Predominately this means that you appear for certain key words on Google. You pay a small price, normally pence or cents to appear for certain key words that you define. You only pay when your link is clicked.

What this means is that you're only paying for qualified leads that are actively searching for your product or service.

If you're a plumber, based in Manchester, one of your key words could be "plumbers in Manchester". You could bid 50p for that key word and if someone was to search and click on your link you would pay Google 50p. However, that person then might convert into a paying customer who might pay £50.00 for a boiler service or £2,000.00 for a bathroom refit.

For some industries, Google AdWords works better than others and as such the cost per click (or CPC) goes up. For other industries, it is not so lucrative or perhaps the profit margins aren't as great so the cost per click comes down.

For some reason though, despite knowing this, some small business owners are still scared silly by the thought of spending money on advertising.

One of my clients (we'll call her Sarah), was particularly worried about this. However, when I looked at her business a bit further I saw she was spending money on flyers. The flyers were costing her around about 6 pence for each one. We worked out that half of them would end up on the floor so really it was costing her 12 pence for a flyer to go home with someone. The person then would have to go onto their computer and type in Sarah's web address.

THE MOST IMPORTANT CHAPTER

In this chapter we're going to be going through being sociable. Now it sounds really basic and that's because it is, but this is the number one issue small businesses have when I've spoken to them. This is the number one thing that they do wrong.

The biggest issue that I see when I go out and look at the client's portfolio, the client's social networking presences and they ask me what's going wrong, what am I doing wrong, why aren't people coming from here, I've got 1,000 likes but no one's bought anything off Facebook or Twitter or Google+. What am I doing wrong? They all seem to miss the point about the social part of the network.

Sure there's lots of people on there to sell to – great! But it's not about "selling to", it's about being social, that's what a social network is. You wouldn't walk into a bar and expect to be hassled over and over and over again by somebody saying: "Do you want another drink, do you want another drink, do you want another drink" You've already gone into their bar, you've bought the drink, or a restaurant and you've bought a meal, you don't want someone coming over all the time asking you time and time and time again: "Do you want anything else", "Can you buy this", "Would you want to buy that?" That's what companies are doing on social networks.

They are selling and selling and selling to their customers. And these guys are people that have actually taken the time of day to actually 'like' you on Facebook or follow you on Twitter, or circle you on Google+. These guys 'like' you already, so don't go selling to them. They're possibly (depending on what industry you're in) already customers of yours so you don't need to do the hard sell and you certainly don't need to sell over and over and over again to them. Social networking is not about being a salesman, it's about being social and by that I mean offering content or offering funny bits and bobs that you've found over the web.

It might not be directly back to your site. Send them out to different sites. You've seen a funny video on YouTube? Post this: "Hi guys, just seen this funny video on YouTube, check it out". It's a YouTube link. Ok, it's not going to drive you a direct sale there, but that's not what social networking is about. It's not about driving the sale time after time. If you want to do that move on to AdWords. Move on to a Cost Per Click basis advertising model. That isn't what social networking is about. Social networking is about being social.

So, how do you do that?

Well, I'll use an example here. I worked with a fashion

company who asked me, why they have got lots of likes on Facebook and a fair few followers on Twitter but they were not selling anything. They weren't on Pinterest or LinedIn but they had a decent enough social presence on Facebook and Twitter and they wanted to know why they weren't selling a thing. Quite honestly they weren't selling a thing and when we looked at the data from Google Analytics; there was next to no traffic coming from the social networks and they couldn't figure this out because they were on once or twice a day on Facebook and they were on Twitter five to ten times a day, which for them was perfect. It's different depending on what market you're in, but for them that was about right. One to two times a day posting to Facebook and five to ten times on Twitter.

So they were posting content and so this puzzled me a little bit for all of about two seconds before I asked them: "Well, what were you posting?" Because it doesn't matter, you can post all you like but unless you're posting the right stuff, it's not going to be listened to and you really need to get that content spot on.

So we had a look at what they were posting on Facebook and it turns out that they were posting a different product of theirs – the link to it – and a short one line, two line extract about what it was on the Facebook page and saying "Go check it out". That was it. Every now and again they would put a link or a code up saying: 'Use this today and get 10% off'.

Great, great, get 10% off. That's added value isn't it? If you're on the social network, if you're on Facebook or if you're following them on Twitter and you saw that you get 10% off – great. What were they posting on Twitter? Well they'd automated most of it, which isn't always a bad thing, so every time they put a new blog post up it automatically got posted to Twitter – there's nothing wrong with that in itself.

And then we looked a bit deeper and looked where the other posts were coming from and the other posts on Twitter were coming from (again) links to their products and their "About us" page and their Facebook page. And every single post on Twitter said something along the lines of "We're on Facebook", "Like us on Facebook", or "Have you seen this new product? It came out last week – Check it out". And then there was a link to it. Or they'd be saying: "Quickly, get this – and the link – before it runs out, it's selling out fast". And that kind of goes to prove the point that I was talking about earlier about not selling to your customer.

Now why would you not sell to your customer?

Well, they're following you on the social networks already but it's not them that's following you. This is the way you need to see it. You have been kind of invited into their social group by them. OK?

Now if you get invited to a party you don't start flinging banners around saying "Check my website out" or "Here's a link – go to that" or "Look at this, buy this". You're grateful that you are there and you are nice and you are polite and you have a chat and you might mention your business in passing every now and again if the time comes or you've got something good to say about it. You don't mention it all the time.

So the fashion company, they did offer some good bits and bobs here and there. The 10% off thing, let's start with that. 10% Off and incentives. Should you post incentives to Facebook, Twitter – yes you should. If that's what you do.

There's a whole other debate about whether you should offer incentives. Does it devalue your product? The Groupon effect as I call it.

I went out for a meal with my girlfriend. Iit was a lovely meal. It was on Groupon and it cost us £10 rather than £60. Would I have paid £60 for it – no. Never would I go back there and pay £60 for it. They've had my £10 and I'd go back and pay another £10, I'd pay £20 maybe, but £60 was taking the Michael a bit. I will not go back and pay £60 for what we had.

Now what they're doing obviously is they're bumping up the value of the product to make it look like it's a better deal. But even if they weren't doing it, the fact that I've got it for so cheap, the chances are I probably wouldn't want to pay the full rate ever again. Now if you start offering 10% off or free delivery or buy this and get this one half price, the problem you start having is people that do buy from you then possibly won't ever buy from you again unless you offer a similar discount. It's not always the case but often that's what I see happening.

But you might argue that the people that do buy from you wouldn't have bought from you normally so you were targeting a different clientele. You have to wonder whether it's the clientele you want to actually attract. Do you really want me eating in your restaurant?

I worked with a separate fashion company, a high end fashion company who sold very expensive pieces of clothing. We discussed the idea of doing an offer, offering some money off - about 15% off. It wasn't a lot but it was enough when you got to those prices. And we were talking about the idea of it and I went away and did some research and I came back to them said that I didn't think it would be right. We spoke through why and it turns out when you offer those kind of discounts, yes you attract a younger clientele – for them it would have been a younger clientele once they could actually afford the clothing at that point. But the problem then becomes that that's not the clientele that they want to attract.

If you want to attract that clientele in the first place just cut your price and attract them. Brilliant! And change your marketing. That's not who they were wanting to attract. So we went back to the drawing board and realised that "money off" was not an option so they didn't post any money off vouchers on Facebook or Twitter.

If that's not you, perhaps you work in an industry where the 'money off' advertising is notorious. You take a rate card and you half it. Most ad rates are ludicrous and you'd expect to only pay about half. So if you work in that kind of industry it might be an idea to say 20% off your rate card.

Use 'money off' very, very carefully. It can be great for you social media but you just need to take a step back and look at the business aspect of that a little bit closer. And only you'll know that because only you know the business. So if you know it does and you do it all the time anyway, fine go ahead.

What about products? Should you be linking products? Should you be linking to your products from Twitter and Facebook? Well yes you should. I know I went on earlier about saying how it was terrible and it's a terrible idea to ever do that. And it was terrible what the company in question were doing. But they were ONLY linking to them. They weren't offering anything else. So, yes link to your products. Tell people about "we've got a new T-shirt out – have a look at it", "What do you think of our new design of jeans?" That is fine; that's great in fact because you're telling people that like your business and like your clothes already, you're telling them that you've got some new stuff out, but most importantly, you're asking for their opinion.

What it isn't good is when you start telling them about the old stuff. They already know about that. So you've got to be really, really careful about how often you post about that. It's all about getting a balance and you'll see that as we go through, it's about getting the balance just right. And that's where the best social media campaigns get it, it's just the right balance.

So we've covered off "money off vouchers". If it's your industry, go for it. If it's not, don't feel as if you have to do it just because it's on social media. You don't.

We've covered off your products. Should we be linking to our products – yes we should if it's good quality content. If it's new, if it's interesting, if something's happened with it. Don't just link to it for the sake of linking to it.

So what about other stuff? What else should you be linking to? Should you be linking to your "About us" page? Yes, maybe but most people would probably know about that already so go easy on it. What about stuff like other people's pages? Other people's content? I would say that yes you should go for it. That is brilliant. That's the kind of stuff that people would follow you for. You're offering your audience something new. Something worthy of their time. That's the kind of thing that will get you some true fans.

Now, what you need to visualise here is your market; your audience; your target demographic. What do they like? Well maybe you're a jewellery company, maybe you sell boilers, maybe you're in the technology industry. Whatever you do, what you need to do is work out who your target audience is, who is Mr Joe Blogs for your industry.

Once you've got that person you can start to paint the picture about what else they might like. It's probably very similar to what you like considering you're both into the same kind of industry.

So if your target market is women who buy jewellery, aged between 30 and 40, you might find they are spending an awful lot of their time bringing up young children. So if you see a video about somebody else's children being a right pain in the bum or anything like that – just as an example – sharing those kind of videos that your target audience possibly haven't seen but you know they'll love will work wonders. It's the same with articles and things that are posted on news websites. If they're going to be interested in it there's no reason why you shouldn't be posting to your Google+ about somebody else's content. That actually makes you better than your rival who is only posting about theirs. Do you see where we're getting here?

We're not just posting about our stuff. We are being a person. We're being sociable.

When you talk to people, you don't just talk about yourself. You talk about other things, you talk about stuff you heard on the radio on your way into work. You talk about stuff you saw on the internet, all of that kind of stuff. That's being social and that is what you need to do on a social network – being social. It's really easy when you get your head round it but so many people don't understand.

So it's just about being social and seeing those bits online and aggregating them and making it so that perhaps people didn't follow you in the first place have a reason to. Bringing in all these different elements and creating a newsfeed of information of news, funny videos, inspiring articles, things like that from all over the web, pictures, audio, everything like that. Commenting on the latest TV series…

If you can provide unique interesting content the people wouldn't have otherwise heard of you kind will see what you do as a service above and beyond what you need to. So you're providing them with something else other than just the jewellery or the jeans or the technology that you supply normally to your customers. You're giving them something else. And that is what social networking as a whole is about. And that's how to make a great social network and a great social network feed.

WHAT NEXT?

So you've (almost) reached the end of the book. You've successfully followed it through and are now looking at a great-looking Google+ page, with a fair few fans that are growing every week. You've cracked the biggest social network and you want to know what to do next. This section of the book tells you exactly that. So without further ado...

Measure Your Google+ Success

If you're going to set up a Google+ page, it's probably wise, in fact it's definitely wise to make sure you're tracking your efforts and measuring your progress. By this I mean, analytics; the big scary A-word that many small businesses and entrepreneurs fear. After all, your expertise lies in plumbing or cake decorating not in analysing data. However, being able to accurately determine how your campaign is going is vital to the overall success of your Google+ marketing campaign. Don't worry though, I'm not going to bore you with hundreds of different ways to measure your Google+ efforts and I'm not going to scare you by going into pivot tables and spreadsheets. Whilst you can do some pretty amazing things with the likes of Google analytics, Microsoft Excel and a few pivot tables; this book is called Google+ business basics and I'd like to keep to the basic nature even in this rather advanced section of the book. With that in mind, the following tools and ways of measuring your Google+ success are by no means exhaustive, however they do give you a nice overview for just when you're getting started. As I said, you're the plumber or the cake decorator or the chef who just so happens to be having to do some social media marketing on the side. I'll keep that in mind and I've kept that in mind for this next section.

So, for measuring your efforts on Google+ I'd like to highlight two tools to you. The first one is one that I've mentioned already and its called, buffer. Buffer was the tool that we spoke about that allows you to schedule in updates and buffer posts. Well it's got another trick up its sleeve as well, and that is its really simple and easy to understand analytics. Along the menu of buffer, there is a tab for each account that says reports. Click it and you'll get to see a breakdown of each post that you've sent out through buffer. You can see how many plus-ones it got. You can get a very quick overview of what does work and what doesn't work for you. It might be that quotes work really well and your Google+ followers love reading them. It might be that they prefer links though. That is the whole point of using these analytical tools, to find out what works and why it works. Buffer is a great tool for this and again is available on their free plan. There is a paid for version for businesses which does link into your Google analytics account, however it is a little bit more advanced so I'm not going to go into that here. Like with anything in this book though, if you want some more information on it feel free to give me an email and we can discuss it in more detail. My e-mail address is at the end of this book.

The second piece of software that I'd like to recommend for analysing your Google+ account is called Steady Demand. If you head over to Steady Demand you can set up a free trial or you can just opt for the paid version if you're confident in it and get clicking. It's a tool that you can't really do anything wrong with and for that it gets a massive tick in the box for me. It's really simple to use as well, you can do a Google+ page audit, which will audit your page and give you suggestions on ways you can improve it. For me this takes basic analytics one-step further. Rather than just providing you the data it offers you actionable advice from it. Just be warned though that this is a piece of software offering you this advice not a human being with real world experiences, so take it with a pinch of salt.

So finally, those are the two pieces of software that I recommend for analysing and improving your Google+ account and campaign. As I mentioned though, these are only some of the basic tools out there and there are more being released every day; with updates to existing tools and add-ons to others. If you're using a tool already that you think is great and is working for you, I would thoroughly encourage you to carry on using it providing of course that it is actually working for you. Whilst it's not a piece of software I do recommend another tool for analysing your Google+ marketing campaign. It's a tool that everyone has free access to at any time of the day. It's called your own common sense. Sometimes we can all get caught up in the numbers, how many followers, how many likes, how many hits and how much traffic, organic paid, CPC, PPC. Sometimes we just need to take a step back and look at it from a human perspective. This is what I like to do every six months with my clients. Sit down and have a look at how it's going, have a chat about the marketing campaigns that I'm running with them and see if there are any glaring errors. Of course I never try to manipulate search algorithms or marketing loopholes, but sometimes even the best of us get caught up chasing the numbers. So my final piece of analytic software for tracking your Google+ marketing success is your own common sense. Use it wisely.

Optimising Your Workflow on Google+

The way I like to work is to utilise a number of free and paid web apps. Firstly I start with Feedly. Feedly is available as a free web-app or there is a premium version too. You don't need the premium version though, in order to do what I use it for, although it is beneficial. In Feedly you can set a number of websites, blogs, newspapers, those sorts of websites to feed your Feedly account. Feedly will then collect every new article and blog post, posted to those websites. What it means that you can all of the websites that you enjoy reading and keeping up to date with, whether it be from a business point of view or a personal point of view, you can read all of those articles in one place. You don't have to go off to each website individually and see what new posts they've added, which is very time consuming. Feedly also supports folders so you can bundle in together all the news from your business industry into one folder. You could then have a folder set up for personal news. To give you an idea of how I use mine, I have a folder set up for business news with websites like Entrepreneur and Fast Company in. I have a lifestyle folder with websites such as Life Hacker and The Four Hour Work Week (the four hour blog) feeding it. I then also have an SEO folder with websites such as Moz and Site Visibility feeding it. Of course, I have a social media folder too with websites such as Social Media Examiner and Social Mouths. And finally I have a technology folder with websites such as Engadget which helps me keep up to date with the latest news and products coming out in the tech industry which might influence social media or SEO, which is what I need to know for my business. This is how I work, it may be very different for you, but have a play around with it because I do feel that Feedly is one of the most powerful tools to curating and collecting useful content that you can share with your users on social media easily and quickly.

The second piece of software I use is called Buffer, and the excellent thing about Buffer is that it works really, really well with Feedly. When you read an article in Feedly you can press the buffer button and it will send it straight over there. But what is Buffer? Buffer allows you to connect your own social media accounts and post directly to them without having to go to Facebook, Google+, Twitter or LinkedIn individually. What this means is that you can send the same message to all of your social media accounts really, really quickly. There is also a function that allows you to buffer your posts. So perhaps you see three great articles that you want to share with all of your Twitter followers, but you don't really want to share them all at the same time. Ideally you want to stagger those posts and updates so there's more chance of them being seen. The last thing you want to do is share five posts at 10 in the morning and nothing for another three days. What Buffer allows you to do is set times that it will post to your said social networks. So if you tell Buffer to post at 10 in the morning 1 in the afternoon and 7 o'clock at night, it will only ever post at those times, even if you load in 20 updates to post. Those 20 updates will be spread out over the following week. Those updates will go out at 10am on the Monday morning, if you were to Buffer them all at 9am in the morning lets say. The second one would then go out at 1 in the afternoon, the third one 7pm at night and so on.

There are more complicated tools and more advanced tools than Buffer that I personally do use, however in a book that's aimed at getting the basics right I don't think it would be right to suggest them here. There's nothing wrong with them but they do get a little bit advanced and can be a little bit confusing for a first time social media user. That's why I always recommend Buffer as the first tool that you should use when it comes to social media posting. It's really simple to use, it's got a lovely interface and it's free. Again there is a premium version, which is great if you want to load in loads of posts, however for most people the free version will suffice. There's also a reports tab in Buffer, which gives you some really nice, top level analytics, which can help you make decisions quickly on what works and what doesn't when it comes to posting on your Google+ account. As you may have noticed I haven't just been talking about Google+. Buffer and Feedly work extremely well with Facebook, Twitter and LinkedIn as well. So if you're on those, you can combine them all up together and save yourself a good few hours a day. Combine it with Feedly and you've got excellent content that doesn't take you hours to produce. So combine Feedly and Buffer with a schedule of postings maybe in the morning and evenings. When I say posting in the mornings and evenings, what I do is look through Feedly on my phone, on my Iphone, I read the articles that interest me and I Buffer the ones that I think are really great to my social media following. That's how I keep my Google+ account topped up with engaging and relevant posts and that's how I stay on top of my Google+ account campaign.

Building a Blog

Blogging can be an excellent extension to your Google+ marketing campaign. In fact, as a stand-alone marketing platform, blogging is one of my favourites. In the online world, websites are built on content – that's what search engines can see, especially written content. So a blog is an excellent way of providing some extra content to your website. It's also an excellent way of defining yourself, your brand or your business as experts within the market. The reason for this is simple: if your blog, which has been active for say eighteen months, posts regular, informative, on topic content that helps the end user they will see you as more than just somebody that takes their money. They will see you as an expert – the people that they go to when they have a question that needs answering.

As such, blogging can be one way of defining yourself, your brand or your business as experts within your field. It's also an excellent way of feeding your Google+ account or any other social media account with fresh content that is engaging for your followers. A lot of my clients comment that they find it difficult to find engaging posts or come up with interesting topics for social media content. A blog can help alleviate this. Every time you post a new article to your blog, that automatically becomes a new social media update.

Learning LinkedIn

LinkedIn is one of the fastest growing social networking sites, whose focus is on connecting people with their business associates, clients, and former colleagues at work. Launched in 2003, LinkedIn has been uniquely known to network people professionally.

But who says it is only limited to professional networking? With greater functionality brought by its new features, LinkedIn is currently being used by numerous entrepreneurs to expand their online business and market their products. Creating a LinkedIn profile is a wise move to allow your business to business (B2B) marketing to reach a new level of effectiveness upon entering the new era of data-driven marketing.

Since LinkedIn offers a business-oriented and update-based platform, B2B marketing can highly benefit from its faster company promotion and more enhanced visibility. LinkedIn can be an exceptional marketing strategy to allow potential customers to research your company and see if they are interested in doing business with you. In return, you may also conduct research on other companies to discover competition, potential partners, and new suppliers to better know your position in business. Through LinkedIn, you may assess your strengths and weaknesses as you compare your standing with other business establishments and create a special marketing strategy to climb on top of B2B Marketing.

LinkedIn also offers a variety of features that can increase the overall appeal of your business. The redesigned 'Company Page' allows you to share updates and reach your target audience, which are essential elements to build a better business that may lead into a deeper relationship between you and your clients. With its streamlined design, you and your client can search through a more organised category of information, such as company news, career opportunities, products and services, brands, career goals, and insights. Through the 'Company Follow Widget', you can also drive people into your company profile and make new, valuable connections. More marketing features such as the 'LinkedIn Signal' and 'Skills Endorsement' tabs increase the coverage of your company by allowing you to monitor LinkedIn feeds, communicate with first-degree connections, and allow others to endorse you based on your specific expertise. Once endorsed by other users, you will have higher chances of selling your products, gaining more customers, and establishing consumer trust. Like Facebook, its new 'Banner' photo allows you to display your company logo or company cover to establish an identity on LinkedIn, which adds to the branding possibilities.

The LinkedIn Company Page, which can now be accessed through iPhones and Smartphones too, poses a great advantage to mobile users. Business professionals coming from America, Europe, India, and China who are reliant on mobile technology can access LinkedIn and respond to client needs wherever they are. This feature paved the way to a more speedy response system, making potential buyers stick to specific businesses online.

At present, LinkedIn records more than 152 influencers, many of whom are prominent figures such as Barack Obama and LinkedIn's owner, CEO Jeff Wiener. With these people on your connections, your story can be more than just an update. Applications like videos can also tell your company story and create a multimedia experience with other users. When told in the right way, your story can also serve as an inspiration and create a deeper connection with your clients.

LinkedIn is considered to be the home of business professionals, where people do business at a professional level. When it comes to introductions and updates, users observe stringent LinkedIn etiquette to maintain professionalism. With less personal gossip and extra-careful users when it comes to product reviews and comments, B2B marketers can rest easy, safe in the knowledge that LinkedIn offers a safe and secured environment.

Pinning your hopes on Pinterest

The latest trend of business today is obviously towards the online realm. Haven't you been reading the book? In moving from the traditional buy-and-sell technique to the most impressive online marketing strategies, small business have taken advantage of social networking to gather more visitors and boost sales.

Recently, Pinterest has been gaining a lot of attention from small and large businesses alike. Pinterest is the third fastest-growing social networking site next to Facebook and Twitter. Its visually oriented platform gives a unique appeal to products and is helpful for targeting specific clients. With over 14.9 million unique visitors, Pinterest can be a good asset to enhance your online business.

There are many ways in which Pinterest can help enhance your online business. Although it may not be quite as popular as Facebook and Twitter, Pinterest's visual approach has captured a specific type of person, which you cannot find on other social networking sites.

It can be the best venue to run contests and engage with customers in a personal and cost-effective way. After creating a business account on the site, you can 'Pin' photos of your product offers, coupons, freebies, and other exciting offers like trips and raffle draws. Since the site has higher work vitality, your pinned images have higher chances of getting reppined, and therefore reaching a wider audience. Surveys show that 10% of shoppers who surf through Pinterest are more likely to buy products that have authentic and fascinating product photos pinned on a Pinterest business page.

Aside from merely maintaining a blog site, you can also use Pinterest to spread the name of your product by pinning interesting pictures. You do not have to write lengthy articles, create call-to-action statements, or experiment on catchy phrases, which are already very common today. With Pinterest, you let photos do the talking for your products and services, and get customers in less than a minute.

Like Facebook, Pinterest also allows users to follow your company or comment on your page. You can use this as an advantage to connect with potential customers, build stronger relationships with your regular clients, drive more targeted traffic, collect valuable information from customers, know their shopping preferences, and respond to certain queries quickly. You can also place the link of your website along with your pinned photos to lead people to your official site. With limited characters for product description, Pinterest allows clients to focus more on your product images and has become a real visual hub.

Pinterest is especially perfect for companies targeting females. Studies have shown that many online female shoppers do not spend too much time reading product reviews and are more interested on surfing through a variety of fun and charming product images. If you're particularly looking to target females, you can take advantage of Pinterest to market your decorating ideas, wedding ideas, fashion and accessories, and recipes through attention-grabbing and mouth-watering pictures. Handy crafts, make-ups, perfumes, and custom clothing are also a perfect match for Pinterest. Not wanting to stereotype, pictures of cars, the latest DIY tools and beer could also be equally at home on Pinterest!

Pinterest is designed and aimed at connecting professionals. Thus, having an account on Pinterest will help you connect with other business professionals, public figures, and other influencers who may potentially help publicise your business. To raise awareness about your company, you can start following big names and popular figures. If they follow you back, you automatically gain a big plus point to your marketing strategy.

Pinterest can be the best place to expose your brand to a larger audience, attract new followers, and engage with your loyal customers at a whole new level. Unlike other social networking sites, Pinterest provides the safest venue to market your product. Since most members are professionals, you can expect more refined comments that will help build your product's image as a whole.

Trying out Twitter

Twitter is the second largest social networking site, and has become an integral part of many people's daily activities. Internet-savvy folks usually use it to announce what they are up to and update people of their whereabouts. Some people also use it to share thoughts and inspirational quotes, promote their photo journals, and gather traffic for their blogs. Business professionals and entrepreneurs have also taken advantage of Twitter's versatility to connect with potential customers, increase engagement with their devoted clients, and boost up their branding strategy.

Twitter helps entrepreneurs enhance their online business in a myriad of interesting ways. It can be the best venue to create a richer experience for your audience through: visual branding, prominent featuring of the most recent updates, and encouraging more traffic to visit business campaigns, news, and other offers. With exceptional functionality and countless potential followers, it could be the key to your business's online marketing strategy.

You can start by creating a business profile to customise your brand and create awareness about your products and services. Since your profile is automatically set as public, other users can view it without joining or logging into Twitter. Every day, your profile page can be seen by thousands of potential buyers - half of them may become your avid fans.

There are three ways you can enhance your Twitter profile to increase your followers and promote your company. First, you can communicate with more users by sharing significant updates. You can use 'Hash Tags' to highlight your products and '@username' to guide customers to engage with influencers and lead clients for a more exciting brand experience on your profile page. Secondly, you can take advantage of its limited characters - every Tweet can offer exclusive content in small amounts, such as product launches, breaking news, new offers and promotions, and real-time messages. Thirdly, you can Tweet a link, video, or photo of your own products or services from a partner provider. The more interesting your Tweets are, the more chance there is that your content could be re-Tweeted by your followers. Re-Tweeting is a significant feature of Twitter that will relay your product or message to a wider audience beyond your initial fan base, which is excellent for expansion and growth.

Even with an existing Facebook account, you can have

Twitter as your second supporting strategy to promote your brand. With a marketing strategy that is easy to adapt from Facebook, Twitter can be the key to driving your business endeavours forward at a whole new rate. Like Facebook, you can use Twitter to help clients solve their problems, answer relevant questions, share practical tips, and give quality advice. By using short yet catchy phrases, you can also lead a specific crowd of people from Twitter to your Facebook account and create a back-to-back marketing strategy that will make clients stick to your business. Complete with blogging and micro-blogging tools, Twitter can also help build your brand's identity. Another thing that you can do with the site is connect with top supporters and prominent influencers who may potentially increase your business appeal, and increase your engagement across different cultures and continents.

When you're using Twitter, you have to remember an important element known as 'efficiency.' It is important that you share the core values that set your company apart from others; create a business page that reflects your corporate visual identity, and Tweet on a daily basis so as to give your clients an idea of what is happening. Achieving a good Twitter strategy coupled with this element can make your Twitter account an outstanding social networking site to sustain brand loyalty from target customers. Combine it with Facebook, and we're on to a winner!

Other Resources

There are millions of websites on the Internet, many of

them claiming to have the best advice for those looking for Facebook business tips and tricks. We all know however, that these websites are not all as legitimate as others. The following list offers itself as an initial guide for further research and advice, but please do bear in mind what I mentioned in my TED talk. If you find a resource that is talking about your customers as if they were a piece of meat, please close the browser window and send me an email instead. I'd rather help each and every one of you individually, than to let you go implementing terrible advice from somebody who couldn't care less about you, or your customers. Anyway, here's my list of places that are (fairly) reliable. If you spot any bad advice, let me know, and the list will be shortened in the next edition!

Lewis Love – lewislove.co.uk

Likeable Media - likeable.com
Moz – moz.com
Social Media Examiner – socialmediaexaminer.com
Site Visibility - sitevisibility.co.uk

This list is by no means exhaustive and you may find that I've missed out your favourite book or blog. If this is the case, I do not apologise. This is my book, not yours!

A Few Final Words (AKA: FREE LUNCH)

This book was a long time in the making. I wanted to steer clear of the typical marketing books that treat customers as meat, instead focusing on the broader picture. I've spent a lot of sleepless nights, drafting up notes, going through chapters with my assistant and editor (both of whom are incredible) and I'd really appreciate it if you could spare a moment to review my book on Amazon.

I would however, kindly ask you to contact me first before leaving any negative review. If you think I've missed something out, or you wanted to know a bit more about any one of the examples I've given, please get in touch and I'll be more than happy to expand upon points, along with a note to include it in further revisions. You can email me at:

info@lewislove.co.uk

Of course, I'd love to hear your opinions on the book if you loved it too! It would be great to hear your story, and be able to offer you specific, personal guidance. You've just read my book, the least I could do is offer you some friendly advice! After all, it's all about being sociable, isn't it?

Thank you for reading my book. I hope you've enjoyed it as much as I enjoyed writing it. I intend to write more books on the subject of social media and business. I'd love to let you know as and when these become available and be able to offer you an exclusive discount. Just get in contact with me to let me know your thoughts on this book, and I'll add you to my list of favourite people to contact upon future releases.

Thanks again for reading, and good luck!

OTHER BOOKS BY LEWIS LOVE

Facebook Business Basics: The Jargon-Free Guide to Simple Facebook Success

The Amazon Bestseller is the ideal companion for conquering the largest social media platform. It also offers good advice for social media marketing in general. The book doesn't promise you 1,000 'Likes' overnight. In fact, it preaches almost the opposite. Think about what a 'Like' is worth to you and your business. What will 1,000 unengaged fans bring? Not much.

Instead, this book looks at how best to engage with the fans you currently have, so when your page does grow, you'll be in a better position to reap the rewards.

Twitter Business Basics: The Jargon-Free Guide to Simple Twitter Marketing Success

Twitter Business Basics is a must-read for every small business owner, whether the social-sphere is a new and bewildering place, or somewhere you have yet to use to its full potential.

Trying to sell your product, engage with customers or gain followers all in 140 characters or less - sound impossible? It doesn't have to be. Twitter Business Basics guides you through all aspects of the Twitter-sphere with humorous anecdotes and real-world examples – and absolutely NO confusing jargon. Author Lewis Love explains terminology, dispels myths and provides actionable advice for a successful Twitter marketing campaign. Most importantly of all, Lewis reminds us that people join Twitter to be sociable, NOT to be sold at.

Help is at hand; followers, profit and growth are yours for the taking. Get your copy and start your success story today!

ABOUT THE AUTHOR

Lewis Love is a new media consultant based in Derbyshire, UK. Originally from Essex, Lewis worked on the breakfast show of a radio station for 18 months before travelling around the world. Upon his return, he moved to the midlands to study Media Studies at the University of Derby. He was the student representative for his course for three years, and in 2012, he was awarded the University of Derby Award Student of the Year for his work with local businesses. Since then, he's worked with start-ups in the fashion industry, multi-national and multi-million pound corporations, advising, educating and occasionally amusing them on how best to implement digital marketing strategies and enhance their online presence.

Besides his work online, Lewis enjoys spending time with his girlfriend, Emily, whom he lives with in Derby. He's an Arsenal fan, although he kindly asks you not to hold that against him, and he enjoys a craft beer from time to time; produced by smaller, passionate breweries, of course.